OTHER PEOPLE'S LIVES

OTHER PEOPLE'S LIVES

CHRIS HUTCHINSON

Brick Books

Library and Archives Canada Cataloguing in Publication

Hutchinson, Chris, 1972-
    Other people's lives / Chris Hutchinson.

Poems.
ISBN 978-1-894078-75-7

    I. Title.

PS8615.U823O84 2009   C811'.6   C2009-902302-4

We acknowledge the Canada Council for the Arts, the
Government of Canada through the Book Publishing Industry
Development Program (BPIDP), and the Ontario Arts Council
for their support of our publishing program.

The cover image is "Night City #4" by Joseph Siddiqi.

The author photograph was taken by Meghan Martin.

The book is set in Sabon and Bliss.

Design and layout by Alan Siu.

Printed and bound by Sunville Printco Inc.

Brick Books
431 Boler Road, Box 20081
London, Ontario N6K 4G6

www.brickbooks.ca

For Anne Grant

Contents

2

3

4

Prologue and Directions

To coax me out
from winter, praise
the newborn fingers
of magnolia uncurling
from their husks.

—∿—

Why resist
the weightless
pleasure, promises
unanchored
as gymnastics
on the moon?

—∿—

Mark each passing
scent, *mildewed* and *sweet*
belonging to the bluish
moisture of your breath.

—∿—

Never mind the fuse
that lit and sped
your journey,
the rills of traffic
echoing and flanked
by the isolate
vacant tracts.

—m—

Note the distant
peaks of rooftops
gathering in the elvish
shapes of fog—

—m—

Now moving alone
inside the radiant
prison of my body,
squeeze your eyes
almost shut.

1

English Bay (Vancouver)

An ingenious wind combs the ocean's surface back
and forth, folds it to black-and-white
piano keys.

The mountains on this coast are not Glenn Gould's
hunched shoulders—though let's say the city hums
in homage to his ghost.

Inside a late March sun, gulls flicker and flash—synapses
of a gifted mind? I wish I were a lone disciple,
or at least an audience of one.

But perched everywhere, the anonymous busts of others
like me: shivering romantics, far from genius,
staring out to sea.

Other People's Lives

Day appears through
a sieve of dust, through a maelstrom
of institutional schemes and designs,
as other people's lives kaleidoscope,
a whirlwind of butterflies, photogenic
as a nation-state, perpetually
childlike—

Night appears through
tear-translucent glass, through insinuations
of blue and the spiritless quality of ice,
as other people's lives glitter and slip,
beads of mercury beneath your
fingertips, or a keyboard
of fireflies—

The Man Who Lives in the Gazebo

The man who lives in the gazebo in the park in this
ineloquent metropolis—we've dreamt he has nothing
but what the rain gives him in his sleep: riches
of a presence, fingers tapping, silver-ringed;
what a child hears of voices, pure plash
of a cadence loosed from sense. This morning,
work-bound strangers mutely trampling
the many-eyed, the dew-decked blades of grass
step around him, living shadows, unrepentant
in their trespass. While across the bay the city
clears its throat but rarely speaks—as language
prefers to find us while we sleep: words
whose meanings fold in on themselves,
on waking, shut the door.

Homeless

You weren't here, the morning light streamed
inside the mist-hazed park where mushrooms
flared like fleshy bells. I almost believed
my mind had grown tendrils and bloomed.

Old women disguised as crows stuttered past,
jigging upon the sleeping city's hip bone,
flitting between the horizon and beer cans
coated with the aspic glow of moonstones.

Drunk, you slept here once, then withdrew—
your mind sticky as a wound, reopening.
Poor pupil of homelessness, you never knew
delirium could become your dwelling—

yes, a place of twisted hues, of doubled sight,
but a house just the same, built of light.

Café Poem

From the northeast corner of the room
came the slant, circumspect glances of enemies
disguised as friends. This city is a forest of the mind,
said our barista in passing, her voice glittery
as a polished spoon. How I wished
I could light her cigarette in CinemaScope,
outside in the *noir* of fog and heady violins—
but those days are over, remarked the coffee
to the cream. You know, I said, I'm often here,
happily bathing in a stream of disinterestedness,
when some owl-eyed child appears, miraculously
tying and untying the knots of his fingers whilst
whistling the tune of a rusted hinge. Such disbelief
is my body suspended, the kid will invariably say—
cheekily pointing the arrows of his cheekbones
towards my treacherous friends whose smiles
all light up like knives beneath
the fluorescents.

A Room without a Door

A room without a door.
Four walls without a window.

Enclosure I fear as fact—fact
which says the body is nothing

but abstract, not a fixed source
of light. Yet the problem isn't earth's

soft penetration, the susurrus
of autumn's piecemeal descent,

it's this mélange of blood,
rust, and sand, this morphing

by the moment, what I tumble
continually from and into—

such wistfulness, the gravity
of feminine hands unfolding

where undercurrents of breath
unlock a series of fascinations,

each embedded in each,
fidelity rooted in desire,

or like a coin-heavy, copper-coloured key,
ordinary as the name I keep.

I Keep a Name

I keep a name, ordinary
as a coin-heavy, copper-coloured key,

desire rooted in fidelity,
or embedded in each

series of fascinations
where undercurrents of breath

unfold like feminine hands—
such gravity, the wistfulness

I tumble continually into and from,
this morphing of each moment,

a mélange of sand, rust, and blood,
autumn's piecemeal descent,

its susurrus and soft penetration
of earth. Yet the problem

remains, how the body's
unfixed source of light is nothing

but abstract. Says who? Says fact,
and fact I fear as enclosure,

as four walls without a window,
a room without a door.

Vocation

Somewhere floats emptiness,
untwisted space, voluminous cavity

in the air which is the air not rushing anywhere—
just stillness, hovering pure, suspended

like a word bubble where nothing is written,
where nothing is intuition adrift, his thought

before it is thought, something less
than an inkling, yet infinitely more;

then it becomes what the wind aimlessly expatiates
in its countless sibilant and indecipherable tongues, invisible

as the fuel time runs on, what lengthens the ash
of his abandoned cigarette, replenishes the many breaths

he's sacrificed conflating piety and righteousness,
counts each drop which falls and pools as ink

inside the basement of his insomniac revisions;
and then—after every measure has been dissolved

and each utterance merged into a seamless monoculture
of exhausted consent—it reveals his transgression with

dreamlike whispers before an assembled jury
of his fears; so it is whatever, wherever, whomever

it is—though it's not within his power to charm
or possess; such knowledge belonging

not to him, but only to what the invisible knows
of itself, and to the sound of wind at night

moving through the trees: premonition's stir,
or just a crowd of *hushes* in the leaves.

Entertaining

Tonight, your friends will come
with masks of coloured smoke,
butter-tongued admonishments,
promises punctuated with the sucking of breath,
winks like flies drawn to sweet liquid,
smiles unflinching as department store lights,
and an assortment of feelings preciously bright as those
lacquered knick-knack miniatures designed to comfort
the elderly in their provisional rooms—all of which
will add up, in the final, sensuous equation,
        to the compulsive-in-you's weird abundance,
            to you-the-bamboozler's bogus largesse.

Then, after dinner and too many
drinks, tightly shutting your eyes as if to choose
your sins, curled up like a fiddlehead, your skull
bowed to the pyramid of your knees,
you will recite:
        My friends, we must never make known
what we know, that any attempt at viewing life
as a series of connected events is either naive
or ill-conceived, and in any case
doomed—

Alas, the theatrical atmosphere
will too easily encapsulate the meaning
of your words: the limelight, unblinking
as a furnace, eating through the stage, and everything
you meant to say rushing into this vacuous pit faster
than your ability to lift your head and acknowledge the looks
scrawled like drunken calligraphy across the brows of your guests.

And so, with everyone anxiously expecting you
to improvise, to jest, to grin like a martyr at dawn,
how the evening will end
in ill health
                    and fashionable ruin.

Nostalgia

Sneak into the movie theatre
through a side door. In the liquid
dark your sense of self will spike
like a candle flame possessed.

Envision the minute jigsaw
of a wrist, loosening, giving
life to these onscreen
marionettes.

The story's smooth convolutions
becoming a child's drawing of a tunnel maze
where the trick is to arrive
back at the beginning.

As the soundtrack peaks,
the exquisite hairs of your inner ear will quiver
in unison, tiny violinists flying
their bows in the air.

Soon, each frame's ephemeral wake
resembles the vee of phosphorescence
the moonless midnight swimmer
of late August trails behind—

Now imagine,
viewed from below,
another kind of scene:

the swimmer's body like a comet appears
to divide cold space, or like a finger seems
to point the way—although whether it's
"out from" or "to where"
you can't say.

Fin de Siècle

No tears. You can't entreat this feeling
to come forth, to lift from your oesophagus and turn
to fluid grief. Your tongue is chalk as the air
reverberates with the crystal of a wineglass someone
glides a wet thumb along, a hum whose colour eclipses
these thin conversations about sex poorly disguised
as cultivated desire. This all takes place at a soirée
constantly played out in some other time you have
invented, where your present needs have been replaced
by trivial yet deep-seated regrets. As always, your hosts
are dressed in the glow of the well-fed and spiritually
tormented. What no one sees: in the gilded mirror
above the bookshelf where Mallarmé decomposes
to blonde motes of dust, an image appears
of your body as it will soon become, as dark water
light gutters over from a moon made of salt,
a moon of fear, a hollow form the night runs
its cold thumb along—as a single violin distils
its single note across the years.

Metamorphosis

Bees in the holly waft around leaves cut
like denticulate jade. Some nestle into buds
the greenish white of lifeless flesh.
How thoughtlessly you consider death.
It's what you see through like a window, your gaze
threading lozenges of sky, or lost in a haze
of spastic white butterflies, excitedly off
to who-knows-where. Yet a part of you
will soon shake free and flit away,
possessed by the energy of sheer instinct,
antennae buzzing like a tuning fork pitched
above earshot—and your new unfolding wits
will perceive each blossom a thousand times
in the unblinking of your compound eye.

A Name

Written in sand, a name
tickles the serpent's belly
as you maunder like Cain
trailing the first infamy across
salt-kissed landscapes—

Written in steel, a name
burns in its imprisonment
as the necessity of escape
rushes up your spine like flame
along a gasoline fuse—

Written in ice, a name
drifts softly into ellipsis
as winter elides the stubble field,
your every syllable
tinged with frost—

Written in light, a name
speaks your corporeal worth
as dust motes hover like airships
fleshing themselves out inside
a corridor of sun—

Written in sleep, a name
trickles from your mouth
as a scribble of moonlit drool,
a smile you'll never see,
nocturnal smile of your homunculus—

Nineteenth-Century Loner

Collectively
we circle a notion
dignified and upright
as a top hat worn by one whose confidence
in the visible world is grounded in
the invisible.
　　　　　But let's consider him
the same as you and me in the difficulties—
more wind-rippled desert than road map
sketched above his eyes—and in the burdens
he has carried across open midnight parking lots emptied
then flooded with the flare of burning sodium.
　　　　　Let's picture the suburbs at night
conspiring against the ornamental opulence
of the dream-state, and him whispering to
and from the death of sleep recurrently
as waves breaking upon the glassy moonlit sands
where no one goes unless alone and
prone to ludicrous imaginings.
　　　　　Meanwhile, above this scene floats a mist
composed of the many cold eyes
of our own observation. What we see:
the tissue-soft landscape recedes,
sinks and shivers away like a fish caught
and set free, and what's definable
fades into the deep.

The Summer Place

Place of privilege and soft
fate of the imagination gone gently
feral, gone to seed.
       Not far from shore
       a sleeper in a dinghy drifts,
the white tips of his shipped oars
like shoulder blades
propping up a world of blue.
       His dream is spotless as Platonic love, seemingly
       inert as the hub of a spiral galaxy, self-contained yet
rippling outwards in concentric rings of light.
       Beyond, we see his summer
       retreat sheltered by a grove of oak
from the westward, salt-lipped breeze.
       Inside, on windowsills, sea glass
       and prismatic shells of abalone. In every room,
dyed silks and watercolours of local wildlife
decorate aromatic cedar walls.
       Like opening a drawer
from childhood filled with pages torn
from old calendars and illustrated books: digging around
we're sure to find a collection of minor talismans,
papery leaves, old coins, and various stones
whose minerals once shone with a candied lustre
inside the ocean's throat.
       Too soon,
September twilight and the song of crickets—
half trill, half thrum.
       And when the sleeper wakes,
rows to shore, and is seduced
by the natural allure of firelight flickering
above the hearthstone like so many drowning hands—

how many liqueurs shall descend the cupboard,
their labels written in majestic, floral scripts?

Spying through the window,
shivering in our chains,
we'll count each sip.

2

And through a Riddle, at the last—
Sagacity, must go—

Emily Dickinson

Game

So significance, bare-limbed but for a broken wristwatch
peels away its skin where fractals of analysis
and breath unfold. So instead of listening, you cross-talk
as logic weeps and syntax bleeds into ellipsis,

an uncertain trailing off, reaching like phantom limbs
of thought, meaning: the sentence as object can be
opened like a multi-purpose tool—just as whim
can twist into an array of conscious deeds.

So watch your fish tank like TV, so train the cat
to drape itself around your shoulders like a stole.
Is it a game, this semantic shuffle, or that
which gets you to the breakfast table—the goal

not the centre, but life's ironic fringes—
obsessed not with words, but with their hinges?

Continual

The Law of Conservation of Energy states that energy
cannot be created or destroyed, but can change its form.

Kaleidoscopic, refreshingly variable, you
transmute like energy, like water ever-circulating
        as mist, river, monsoon, tears—
this attempt to evolve and increase, old enemy
of atavism, as always, from here on in
        pressing forwards, first erotically into then
fully beyond tomorrow—despite the neon-clad
crossing guards with eyes tripping like traffic lights
        as you steer towards the horizon, mindless
of the stop-sign sun and running
on synaptic combustion and reflex
        desire, on a four-lane highway built
from the smashed-up tombs
of the illegitimately deceased—then
        carried away, riding light's smooth mechanics,
unswerving as the clockwork perfection
of your own perpetual self-
        defeat, you push onwards, leaving culpability
and the credibility of good credit
behind, finally exceeding physical expectations
        as if the body were actually designed
for purposeless sex—hence, long ago,
continual rebirth became Law, the role model
        and drive for every citizen born
under no sign of ill omen, beneath no
hemorrhage-coloured moon, while no breeze
        let slip sibilant half truths, the no one
you would leave behind and the someone you would
become both impatiently waiting,

raring to go, pissed off
at the delay, hovering in the volatile,
aromatic zones of ether and imagining
        below a succession of irresistible affairs
gleaming down there like a row of teeth
in the soon-to-be death-fecund soil.

As It Was

The city was a beautiful day.
Out on the grid, the open grid, vehicles
multiplied a certain domestic resonance.

Signs stopped. Whatever it was they were
thinking moved us, traceries of smoke rising
from the lips of the jackhammer squads.

You'd soon surrender the institutions whereas
I'd pick out conspirators the way the sun
highlights the creases and nipples of cellophane—

but not before we had levitated beyond the merely
quixotic realms of impulse, flesh the texture
of the detachment of swans. Like lovers held

in abeyance, caught out on the esplanade,
wondering if it could rain cats and dogs.

Mining Sapphire

I'd rather reflect the sleep
of twenty castle-shaped clouds—

quiet as an unplanted garden,

a belief saddening
in the saddest of times,

clutching the wine cup without
letting a single telltale drop

insinuate itself like
a crystal of aluminum oxide

slipping down the peacock's
effulgent throat.

In my worst moments alone:

eucalyptus diving in-
to the green lake of itself,

cricket at night cheeping beneath
the floorboards, or me placing a foot

in the valley
in which I was discovered

so tears of blood
might brighten

the medieval statue's cheekbones—
wondering,

what makes the experience
exquisite? Mineral-hard

proof or simply rocks in the beguiled
jeweller's head—meaning

    crushed like light through a chandelier.

Though I'd rather masquerade
as something easier to conceive of,
a designer brooch
amongst the high-stepping set,

sparkling wit of the vehement
intelligentsia—who these days

can afford *not* to invest in their
    pageantry of feelings?

Or an alcove
where the wind shakes its fists

at the remnants of sleep, as I who
was murdered

awake
    spitting seeds of red worth—

No City for Young Victims

Another Claims Examiner with fever-
shakes and a surgeon's scalpel
this town doesn't need.

Not another knuckle on a sporting fist
bled white with first-place obsessions,
cruel as an Old Testament stone.

But rather a clock with fingers
splayed like slithering filaments suggesting
a tactile and sexual nature.

Or a forest of cigarettes for the deinstitutionalized
and, at the centre, for their spiritually malnourished pets,
a mandala of bones. Why?

Because the body both receives and transmits,
an elegant agent for assessment and action
or, in today's case in point, physiognomic revolt—

That is—

if it weren't for this soupy suspension
made from the broth of platitudes and slogans.
If it weren't for this slime-mould bureaucracy.

Then everywhere: palm trees! Green shimmering
pompoms that rejoice in victorious ascent above
trunks wed to the vertical plane of the crucifix.

Now imagine: pain without victimhood
as a commercial by-product, and the streets freckled
with patterns of actual blood, as living.

American Still Life

You have an enemy at last,
        a jewel under water.

Your silhouette unfolds then
billows around the empty room.

Or is it the black searchlight
        of your own attention

which tracks across the windowsill?
Here, the small corpses of flies

arrange themselves, spelling
words from a dead

language. What's not
        inevitable?

Cigarette smoke, empty
beer bottles at the ready, yet tomorrow

will come, and syllables,
smooth as wet marbles

        will shift, slip from your
mouth, crack and shatter

to grains of coarse salt.
Soon, there will be nothing to say,

nowhere left to go without
        guilt.

Pre-sleep, a palimpsest
of valleys and streams—

　　　Then the dream
opens, crackles like footsteps

along a gravel path,
a path from the waterfall

to a fallen nest
of newsprint and

dried blood
　　　wherein

this gelatinous, synthetic creature,
boiled to near bursting,

appears—
　　　such pink rubbery fingertips!

In each pupil, a small
pinpoint of light like a ding

in the windshield of the soul!
　　　Wherein,

with only the smell of burning
wires and a fine spray of nerves

to reveal itself, with its spiny
glances along the rotting window—

as if tracing the fledgling arcs of the most
sadistic of your obsessions...

sadistic
            as in *precious*—

Small Town: Menagerie

He lived among animals who had no concept of despair—
black-and-white cat and chihuahua mutt:
two electrons buzzing an invariable centre.

His station on the human, terrestrial plane lent
a flawed sense of continuity to every
pock-shadowed ceiling at first light.

Troubles like hard-boiled eggs
peeled by cerebral-quick fingers bounced
on the kitchen floor the happy dog

scavenged from. While the cat, sublimely
disenchanted, with a whip of her tail
dissolved the blue static, the cold fuzz

of bygone acquaintances, yesterday's
provincial news. Outside it was a lovely day,
threatening no one. So he would move

into the spaces made from others' movements
and join with the birds breathing through open beaks,
the carnivorous flies, and a summer pox

of children begging in ragged constellations.
Limbs and souls warped and disfigured
from the recent beautifications.

Riddled

What the black helicopters know,
blades snapping like machine-gun fire.

Why such clatter foreshadows the latest
News Report on art's failure
to inquire.

What other sounds?

There are birds I have no names for.
Their songs inhabit the interstices
of my inner life, its family trees,
its weather charts.

Deeper still,
a shadow's breath, disembodied
footsteps, weird shrieks from inside
the theme park, pleasures
self-contained and dark.

Listen: I'm neither
sad nor happy, meaning
I don't know where to go,
or who I'm supposed to be.

Some say my tongue's
a frozen waterfall, its cascade
locked outside of time's
persuasive flow.

Others see it as a runway
for wingless arguments—perhaps
the reason no one cheers whenever I clear
these paisley-devils from my throat.

But as rumours of my death
fester on long after the pedants have retired—
a fertile conspiracy of facts wherein
the worms of fiction grow—

I think: *Silence does not exist;*
and even if it did—

Talking

Being intelligent yet sick the precision of our insights is honed
to a silver point that enters the mind in a self-inflicted pleasure
of pain akin to a syringe piercing the cheerless libertine's vein. Above,

altocumulus undulatus striate slowly west while across the street reflected
white ripples reach like fingers of plague towards the city's east side.
I'm talking about talking endlessly with you about sickness and the mind

stuck in a groove of disbelief, about synapses and lips friable
as scorched aluminum on stinking hot mornings of reciprocal need and
tumid eloquence. It's this friendship based on a love of flamboyant natter,

each phrase itself a mouth full of teeth; anecdotes passed on like
sparkling talismans, precious as the small, intricate, unworkable objects
bequeathed to us in dreams. So sing, my friend, your long complaint,

and I'll grind my organ of ironies or, like a semantic explorer, with a wink,
circumnavigate whole continents of meaning. How we must appear, words
falling from our lips like coins from a bumbling magician's sleeve! But who

can say whether this grackle beetling through the scrub makes the same noise
as a pencil held by a quick-sketch artist whose hand freezes each detail
into its ideal Platonic expression? Suddenly I cannot argue but nevertheless

it occurs to me—as religiously as wind skims the worldly surface
of appearances—that it's only ourselves we can't explain; and this city,
a circus tent of echoing applause and shrieks, each of us desiring a place

at centre stage. Then again, maybe it's the way grief celebrates and grins,
our funhouse visages reduced to shards of laughter; and the fragments
of our love, our strident and tremulous attempts at concealment—

Cross-Eyed

Feathers of milk, or fingers of the elderly;
in the institutional dark, eyes blind as seeds.

Soon the suburbs will overgrow the banks
of these sludge grey rivers, in uniform ranks

trees bow down to the holy, ascendant,
insufferable heat. Now history slants,

breezes across the urban grid, the name
"freedom" anchored like a kite. Locals bathe

where the wound opens, conceivable as light
without an image. A stranger, I alight

on a horizon so indefinable it defines me:
skeletal trees, rows of houses, uneven teeth.

If description belongs to the surfaces of things—
how the mind swerves, disbelieving.

Crosswinds

According to aerodynamics there are
horizontally stacked sheets of glass—

moments, not monuments
the machinating troposphere

at whim deforms. Once we begin,
taxiing at ground zero, each integer

a toehold quickly pixelated
into innumerable Space Shuttle scraps,

we are embraced again,
but by the wrong technology, developed

to help transport people, cargo,
military personnel, and poetics.

Crossover I

Tracing our dream back,
we arrive.

The plum-coloured surface
falls away,

a wilted tongue,
and now we must

simply survive on
how we feel,

fog laced with
threads of smoke,

and this sad
texture which is

the wet clay
of death's

inaccuracy.

Crossover II

If only
an orange-winged light.

If another night's rest meant
all the difference.

If the feeling persists
or spills into the exhausted,

colourless sound
memory makes

as it crosses
the tracks—

Then what
minute perspectives

one's breath
might

confabulate.

Crossover III

Yes, I am my own
poverty and, love,

you are your own
soon-to-be

poisoned prey,
your web adorned

with shucked remains:
faces

at the fringe
of sleep—

how they either
wither away or

widen their eyes,
all teary and

terrified and
strangely

sated.

Someone Else

Almightily alone, I unplug the world,
place the plastic globe on an empty vase
and proclaim the wellspring dry.

My own irony chews me up, spews me out.
Face of a famished war machine! Oily lips
writhing in figure eights.

It's as if someone else
were here, rudely pointing with his eyes,
signalling with his chin, silently asking.

"These drowsy hands," I answer.
Each fingernail, a mouth yawning
in perpetual fatigue. But I will endure,

patient as the enchanted flame that sleeps
inside the match head. I will note each swing
and twist of consciousness, though only to equate,

much later over drinks with persons I have
yet to meet, the fluency of running water
with the vertebrae of coral snakes. Until then,

my only friend on the phone, boastful
as a parade, marches his opinions, all
spit and polish, into my right ear.

The phone is a device which opens me up,
coldly shuts me down. If I could cradle myself
I'd doze to its cosmic tones,

dream in tongues I might one day transcribe.
Instead I gather in what remains of the fabric
of my private life, draw it up around my head,

not a monk's hood, but a tunnel of attention.

Suburban Interior Magic

It's too bad I can't plug the monitor into the grease trap,
my plumber having discovered another word
for victims of botched electrolysis.

Perhaps I'll just bolt the gate and feed the atomizer
its usual baseball fetishes, that is, until there are tap shoes
to incinerate as if having never read *The Pumpkin of Dusk.*

Or if I reorganize these sleeping pills
so that they resemble a skyline boiling with birds
then no one will call about that dairy farmer's polemic.

Though it's likely the spider plant will think it's a spider
the way it's likely the accordion of the future
will resemble an air conditioner.

Regardless, this cat, thinking in binary terms,
thinking *cryptozoology versus philately,*
has again leeched my shag carpet of nutrients.

Tonight, will I wonder how to choose between the comedy
of a pinhole-burnt eiderdown and the anecdote
of a laundry hamper overflowing with Thanatos?

Or will my landlord realize it's high time
to honeycomb my interior again, seeing that
the thermostat is mixing liquid nitrogen

with lemon gin, off carousing with nymphs
and gryphons, regardless of gravity,
despite my New Age sang-froid—

Passing Through

Watching the news in Tucson
through a yellow fog and
the nightlife of East Berlin
descends in rapid spirals, gently
alights on my left pinkie, as always
wearing its tiny fedora.

I'm used to this
as anyone is who's ever hitched a ride
rather than driven his own car
through the drive-thru
of History.

It's what makes me nostalgic
for my other life, the isolate Canadian one
in which I once dissolved
like a cube of sugar inside
a glass of flaming absinthe—

     the artist!

In America our heroes are one
part sweet to three parts villainous,
says my little stoned angel, says
my glittery ghost-twin speaking
its duplicitous mind.

     Such songs
are the ladders I climb, rising
from experience to milky
abstractions, obsessed
with what I'd say

if I were an Italian Master, and this,
Florence in the sixteenth century...

But around here I am
no one and everyone
likes me.

The Way the Day Devolves without You

10.
Through autumn's many rooms,
and shunning the landlord's sun-struck
flint of eyelashes, rays bursting like capillaries.

9.
Through every hour alone, unasked for—
and such quality moments
with the houseplants!

8.
The way desire's predecessor,
lighting a French cigarette, laments
the day we cast our serpentine scripts of light
onto her Saskatchewan riverbed.

7.
The way, out walking today, wrapped up
in the cry of wolves and the scent of impending
rain, I imagine you note each
fallen leaf, each small un-
spoken grievance.

6.
A stranger's palm on your face—
its touch, a cold mirror.
The air, overripe with shadows,
blue tracers of smoke, ritual's
afterbirth, afterglow.

5.
Through October, November, Vancouver, December—
and the walls littered with several unknown
species of flies like the apocryphal
minions of death
gone awry—

4.
Love, if only such moods were the source
of our romantic accord, and not
our quotidian disputes.

3.
Now I see you
peering through my window
like some salivating adjective.

2.
Instead, mount the ladder, the cool
assemblies of your own spent breath.

1.
Ascend.

One Love

Who knows how much time we've spent comparing
ceremonial scars, or listening to the sound of leaky pipes
tapping out indecipherable codes we misconstrued
as tomorrow's way of whispering slippery
promises.

I think you were the first to notice how cold
to the touch and greasy the walls had become,
and what we had previously believed were stars
was only daylight peeking around the edges
of the manhole covers.

Now, either someone somewhere scrapes
a fistful of forks across a smooth mineral surface,
or the noises we try to ignore are of rats scrabbling
along certain moist passageways we plan
never to explore.

It appears as if underground life
has distorted our senses and, even though our eyes
have grown to the size of fists, we can no longer discern
between our own puffs of breath and each other's
wan complexions.

Saturnine, gelatinous, we wobble as one. Bloated
we ripen, a mushroom in the dark. The fetid juices
of our singular body becoming the sacramental sap
we seal in jars and store as provision for what we intuit
as the approaching Spiritual Crisis.

No, there was never a time before. We never lay in bed
and listened through the open window to the entangled sounds
of traffic and crows and chattering passersby—as each sound
never freed itself and spiralled off into a future
where neither of us would ever be alone.

Academe (and Emily Dickinson)

When she came to, they were playing
a harmless circle game—they were saying:
By what process can her process be
revealed? Where's the line between
pedantry and reading between the lines?
If the facts give reason for our cause,
then is there cause for lies?

But now she sees, through the fogged
lens of embarrassment, how the sensuality
of her dream—the one in which the pretty
eyes of a tarred and feathered kangaroo
widen to pools of admonishment—flew
in the face of the assembled congregation
and unhinged the conversation—

Monkey-Man

Serving spoon or
funhouse mirror—

so enamoured with the tool
you sometimes forget

its function: gramophone or
satellite dish, anything

machined, moulded, made:
whatever lasts, not

the object but its task:
what you see, not always exactly

what you get: slide trombone or
shotgun barrel, this place

where uncertainty breeds
potential, where appearances

lay their traps: polyamorous
as a flower, polymorphous

as a glance fraught
with innuendo and subtext:

the way, in 1913, Duchamp schemed
with stool and bicycle wheel:

the way desire defines itself
in the moment before

the application of your will:
weightless as a hammer

at its zenith, then
downswing, decisive act:

that which exists in the hand,
less phenomenological proof

of your own cleverness
than reminder of what

you're striving for: timepiece or
wedding band, or the abstract

work of words themselves: breath
harnessed to sound, sound

fashioned to whatever
meaning suits your need, serves

your fleeting purpose: every
invention, a jerry-built attempt

to nullify the distance
between your reach and what's

forever beyond your grasp:
telescope or microscope, or

even the weapons you turn
upon yourself.

3

Tautologies of Becoming

As the newborn dead
thrown headfirst
from the astral plane

mistake the rushing wind
for a hand to keep them
safe, suspended

(at least this is how
I've dreamt of it, unwilling
to say goodbye:

clouds like doors closing
and unclosing: it seems
absurd to wonder why)

so the living softly
procreate in the mollusc-dark,
creatures curled

in sorrow, devoted
to the world concealed
inside the world.

Notes from the Top of the World

A darkening light, the north
lugging its gold-mine-past towards
the settled abandonments.

Wordless sophistry of a lynx's shadow
ribboning across yellow hummocks of mud.
At the birch forest's edge, the river

steeled for turbulence, each
new bright flex of current bending
to the will of its own resolve.

What desolate ones will inhabit the rooms we fled,
boredom gone to delirium tremens, cities all
pissed into the drains?

Just one road leads away, and away—
encroaching rumours of wildfires,
dream-helicopters of smoke.

What refuge to expect from a wind-
kicked tarpaulin, its inhuman tattoo
beneath the spill of aurora borealis—

No Such Address I

Now standing
on this

ghost-lit
corner

as each
receding

tail light
spills

onto the street
the rain

has polished
to a mirror

as you slip
into

the weathered
measure

of a whispered
phrase

past wanting
to describe

this city
as ellipsis

as mist
describes

this feeling
of having

something
very small

and strange
to say.

Up Above

An airplane's funnelling drone. The sky
uncoils, a rope chasing its anchor
into deep nothingness.

Morning traffic grumbles through
the small snapping-twig sounds of sleet.
And beneath it all the more piteous

version of myself I have forbidden
to speak still grovels in whispers and cries
with what it perceives as her selfish devotion

to a loftier, more autonomous life. Why
do I leave the house? Everything
is January's fault. The leafless trees

are nets for whatever memories fall
from above: an erotic sacrifice or the tragic
birth of some absurdly wingless bird?

The time she shed her newly
purchased black lacy underwear and
threw them out her third-floor window—

a small, reckless disclosure,
quick as a wink's invitation
of risk and possibility.

Believe me when I say that
every love story hinges
on such a moment, swings open

like a trap door.

Veronica Lake: Purgatory

After months of nights of hiding
she finds a way, threads the maze
of a room inverted, light bulbs rising
from their cords like long-stemmed daisies.

Lit by the white-hot filaments
she cannot touch for fear of being burned,
Montreal evaporates. How spent
she is, too hurt to sleep, eyes covered

with moth dust, gulping air
so her mouth appears to be singing—
another sometime denizen of rue Montclair?
Or say she arrives at the beginning

to traverse the western meadowlands
that drink the dying rivers, or drink sand.

What We Think She Sees

In an oval of sunlight
fringed by a scrim of shadows cast

from Japanese maples, a panhandler
sits, legs crossed, head bowed.

A taxidermied raccoon rears beside him,
an upturned, sequin-covered fedora set

in its petrified paws. Across the street,
pigeons throng the library steps like bruises

made by fingertips. Traffic congests.
Each idling car, the shiny segment

of a millipede's body seen only
by the photographer from the roof

of the new condominium she was the first
to inhabit. Before the chemotherapy

she'd dyed her hair a lurid pink,
a bitter jest her friends mistook

for courage. Alone now she resents
her isolation, the distant quarrel

her flesh has become—antimetabolites
brusquely refocusing the lens

of each insurgent cell, morphine
cooing the terms of a false armistice.

The first time she leaves her body,
she sees herself as she sees

the world, the way the mottled shell
of the camera conceals her sexless face.

The second time, let's say she
snaps the shutter, but captures

only a swallowtail butterfly's
calico wing.

Art

He had readied himself for years,
polished his virtuous gaze

in the mirror and professed
to the long-suffering air

his steadfast resolve
to be giving.

He had promised the past—
all which he had once

stolen and squandered,
acting as though grievance

was a form of entitlement—
was a room

he would keep forever
sealed shut.

Ravenous, repentant,
he awaited, in silence,

with infinite patience,
your miraculous living form.

And when you arrived
he became exactly

the one you needed—
the selfless one

who possessed the deep
balm of quiet. Listening,

how he could be so perfectly
there and yet nowhere

at all, close as he was afar
from either ruin

or disclosure.
But knowing, at least,

that desperate is the opposite
of attractive, he smiled,

folded his arms tightly
across his chest, kept sealed

the room where a single point
of darkness held its breath

the way a fist holds
its readiness to strike.

And this he called discipline,
devotion to his art.

So he stood before you
as a conjuror

stands before a mirror
rehearsing his illusory

sleights and charms—and so
did he calmly charm you both,

until, in the end, his calmness
turned to stone,

and made him keep more
secret in himself,

more alone.

Cockroach

What makes this cockroach linger
in the sudden light is something
guiltily human.

Antennae move
like a conductor's arms flailing
at some invisible orchestra—

or are they a pair
of aircraft controller's batons
semaphoring directions
to back off?

No, more like the crossed lines
of a swastika. Nocturnal perdition
sawing its way through
the very walls,

and a violence welling up in me,
a disgust at myself, at something
so vulgarly familiar I cannot
allow it to live.

Slipper in hand,
I deliver my terrible judgment!

Ornament of squalor,
persistent black speck
on an x-ray of the soul—

now your twitching carapace is almost
beautiful, reminiscent

of the fine lustre of expensive cognac or
that old cherrywood dresser I remember
from my grandparents' home,

one of many refinements they couldn't afford
but clung to, even as they endured
the Great Depression
and the War.

Dear Sidewalk

Forever supine,
let's say your life until now
has been laid out
like an unread book.

Gum-riddled, sun-bleached,
rain-sluiced, resilient
groundwork of all my
ambulatory designs.

Before I hit the road,
my foot hit you, the uncertainty
of first steps, of perhaps ever
arriving home again.

Setting out, the path ahead
seemed simple—straight,
then left or right. Yet at times
your ways were labyrinthine.

How the term "street life"
wasn't quite accurate, but
kept you peripherally
in mind.

"Hard knocks" also implied you.
Even the well-heeled
would feel the impact of your
unbending gravitas.

Yes, in the city where I knew you best
I squandered a small quantity
of blood on you, pissed at two a.m.
amidst neon shards of glass.

Today, moon-pocked with age,
weeds grow like superstitions
through your cracks. Though once
your new wet surface lured fingers:

the way I coveted
your soon-to-be permanence
writing my simple equations
of love in your uncured flesh.

Shadow canvas, protean sky's
stillborn twin, ossified, downright,
unmoving—how all you know of me
is transience.

The Invention of the Aeolian Harp

On that night—
disenchanted by the odds
at winning my next game
of solitaire, and annoyed by the many moths
rapaciously flinging themselves against the glare
of my desk lamp's forty-watt bulb, their impacts
mingling with the wind-driven spatters
of rain at my window—
        on that night
I abandoned
my pursuit of a contemplative life
to watch what turned out to be
an awful film, made for TV, wherein
two proportionately dissolute brutes
bear down upon and consume
a tragically meek and naive
introvert—
        which, incidentally, is exactly
the thing I fear: entrapment, an isosceles
of betrayal—though not in love per se,
but in the dangers of walking between
two parked cars, or in the wooziness
of staring too long into a pair of mirrors
angled in such a way that corridors
appear, each depicting an endless row
of solitudes, pointlessly inscrutable
as an equation
of zeros—
        and I'm sure it was
just this kind of self-reckoning
which once mothered the need to invent
the Aeolian harp, an instrument precluding

lyrical genius. Imagine the effortless artistry of wind,
the fusion of vowels in the lover's ear—that is,
until the air becomes still as a vial of poison,
and the lover, deceived, drops soft
and dead to the floor.

Whatever It Was

From Broadway, past maples whispering
where summer breathed its last, I drifted

into Kingsgate Mall, simply to be around strangers
for awhile. There, the multitudes appeared,

heads floating like the pallid, pocked, spongy balloons
left over from last night's celebration,

the occasion for which
no one could recall.

Only the small boy—quietly fascinated
by the mechanical horse, charmed amidst

the sterile and stationary surfaces by the one
machine actually designed for his body's delight—

only his eyes hovered, soft as bees
inside the flower of his face.

Strange, I could sense but not envision those times
I'd felt myself moved to such stillness—back home,

how an old friend called and we recited our usual catalogues
of small grievances, lonely complaints.

And then, for reasons known only to the capricious hand
which charms the weather and occasionally sends us spinning away

from our accustomed selves, how I almost said something
tender, something I'd always wanted one of us to risk

putting into words—as the moment slipped
into the soundless space between us,

simply whatever it was
we so firmly understood.

Just Awake

To describe exactly the pure inhabitation of a single moment,
the pen moving on the page like a dreaming eye, like a bird's wing
adjusting itself to the shifting breeze.

Whose words are these?

So everything goes on and nothing changes.
Spring arrives disguised as winter, a constant moil
of shapeless clouds guttering forever east;

and the robin's small bravado, its apple breast
aglow inside the morning light, the image of love
taking a stupid risk.

Or I'm just awake and waltzing awkwardly to the self-
conscious rhythm of my own
unfamiliar company; dazed

as daffodils on weakened stems
bow their heads; amazed as bright
berries of holly trees pierce the huge

abstraction of the sky, accidentally
poignant as drops of blood
upon an empty page.

And how the pen moves
trying to sing.

Elevation

Snow, mountains, levity. The sky
like a moth-eaten sweater unravels
in wisps of white…

I had not meant
to find myself—not here
in this thin, rarefied atmosphere.

The same city I left behind
awaits, though I expect it will
have changed without me.

I expect it will take me back
like a remorseful lover and I will go into her
as if for the first time.

Because I will have changed.
Lungs turned wings, oxygen-light.
Mind, swept lunar-clean.

Because only these peaks like
sculpted white flame will endure
long after I have descended.

In Passing

Morning finds a man,
wrapped in tarpaulin rags,
rising from his knees.

On his chest
he can still feel the hand
of heat from his careful fire
which has begun to fade
into an arrhythmia of spits and sputters
from the first few drops of rain.

—⁂—

Underfoot,
a typewriter
gone to flora, honeysuckle's
tendril scripts oozing
through its keys,

and a stethoscope
like a necklace laid out across
a bed of sodden leaves.

—⁂—

In this world, in passing,
a weary driver, her third time to the city
since the phantom pains began,

glances
a dark figure wedged
against the abutment—

his torso bowed, black ear tubes
sprouting from his head—

and from within the somatic
rhythm of wipers washing away
the morning rain, she
awakens with the taste
of honey in her mouth—

wondering
if she is still asleep.

—◊◊—

Everywhere, the pathogenic mist of traffic.
Breath of the infirm. Molecules of disease.

—◊◊—

At the clinic, it will be the same:
corridors like metallic strands of light
shunted into a cave—

as her doctor, a man she hardly knows,
this creature whom she will come to understand
as the sole author of her suffering,

speaks a word,
soft and definitive
as a pronouncement of love.

—◊◊—

So unlike her dream of him,
the figure beneath the viaduct
who crouches to hold a stethoscope
against the guardrail's folded steel—

a human shape bent
in either rapture or reflection,
as if listening to the city
inside the city, attentive

to the steady sluice of tires twined
with the echoes of departure.

The Musicologist

The conductor's arms
like a child's untied shoelaces

swing in step with the cadence
of his momentum. While the pianist

who walks a corridor sounding
of wing beats on water moves

with a frailty which radiates outwards
as a single string is plucked

from a concert harp. Will the audience
perceive the harpist as separate

from her instrument, and her fading note,
a third existence, temporal yet forever set

within the history of feeling? No, says a silence
so imperious it may soon create a need

for insurgent forms of art. Which is why
the musicologist hardly sleeps, astonished

inside the gap between his calling
and his livelihood, why

he stands alone each day outside
the monolithic auditorium—as if to listen

meant to wait for someone
who never arrives.

No Such Address II

Hello sodium-lit street. Complicating
rain. Bicycling wind. Gyratory wind-
sexed rain. Hello reflective pools. Ripples

flexed like bowstrings. Ancient
cavalcades of mist escaping streets
known only to those travellers the cold

has led astray. Hello wolf-coloured
smoke, guarding the entranceways,
marking the unseen exits

with your scent. I am the maze
that greets you, the cold that turns you
by the wrist. Each footstep

a question the other answers
with a question. Each breath re-addressed
at the intersection of each breath.

Me

The window
a distilled wind

where the eye
incessantly

roving trying
to see itself

dissolves
falls

through
the proverbial

unblinking
rabbit hole.

On the other
shore I imagine

you the historically
obscured and

tragically
autonomous

observe the world
invert like a room—

walls sheering up
and away

as the blown
crests of waves

hurricane into
and merge

with an aquatic sky's
softer hues—

supposedly where
our secretive

selves might
one day blow

kisses then chase
ornate symmetries

of affection across
an invisible and

perhaps everlastingly
theoretical plane:

that which at once
joins and keeps

separate any
given moment and

our coming
vis-à-vis

our seeing
and being seen

our touching
and being touched.

4

Each man is a half-open door
leading to a room for everyone.

Tomas Tranströmer, "The Half-Finished Heaven"

Cross-Sections

Witness to the invisible frame.
Shocked into a false enlightenment.
Then dial-toned across rivers of static.
Then barrels of oil thrown at prosperity's flame.
Having parted the towers like a postmodern Moses,
the only thing that makes us safe
is the domestic.

I awake in dreams, underground,
alive in the trench the whirlwind carves,
sheltered from politics. Whole families living
in bank vaults, existing on diamonds and gold!
Others sucking marrow from the bones
of scholars until no one's
left to follow.

Why begin again?
Because you are gone—
a flame cut down by wind, a wind
obsessed with consequence, moving through
the body's white-lit corridors, twisting
the tiny ribbon of each breath.
Still, my mouth is open,

gullibly alive in the scented
rooms of hubris, the forgotten
taste of my mother's milk. I admit
I arrived complaining. I had colic for a year.
On each sip of consciousness my stomach
swung on its hinge. But you were gone.
So I began to sing.

I look at my fingernails then touch my nose.
You'd think with all the technology today I
wouldn't need such crude reference points
to locate my existence. But what's true
is the inverted lie. Without me music pours itself
into the funnel of an abyss. Inexorably
the same old wheel gets reinvented, greased.

Impassively falling in love with the passive
voice—this is how the spirit is bled.
I've seen the Grand Canyon from the air,
glanced the titles of classics without taking them
off the shelf. I've gone over this before,
reiterated in the latest styles and forms, my hands
poised, covetous above the thing I fear.

Each day's a notch on the oven dial
the sadistic hand of summer turns. The locals here
wear mirrored glasses with the mirrors reversed!
Was I ever filled with sweetness and courage?
For miles and miles the asphalt unwinds, the river's
evil twin. So is desire your enemy's friend,
goes the jazz of imagined footsteps

slapping the city's impervious skin. So each day
lapses, un-spools each night as I go scheming
ways to continue, safe within and darkly through
an immaterial sublime. But the walls are sweating
and the windows here peer in towards this sheltered
corner of the universe—where I'm in trouble again
with words, and other people's lives.

I'd like to live a harder, faster life
with fewer consequences. It's no miracle
we repent. Every impulse shuddering
in its primordial sleep until, inevitably,
the branch breaks, the cradle falls, and
abstractions swarm the headlines like
columns of soldiers on parade.

Perhaps it is a less human catastrophe
I was truly meant to inhabit, haunted
by twenty-first-century glitz. But now I'd like to be
alone with my mistakes, trust in visions
which arise from acute denial of the senses.
Meaning I'd like to begin again, in poverty,
with some outrageous story.

Form at rest, lassitude of fingers, wrists bent
in repose of narcotic bliss. The head, baroque-
heavy, perplexed. The trick is to stop trying,
let the blood pursue its Faustian musings.
Once, our hands were mouths, our fingers teeth,
and what we desired, always just beyond
our grasp. But lamentation is a sad

excuse for sentiment. Today, something's either
missing or gone to sleep, as if history were finally
tired of coming 'round, leaving us to something
far more sinister: ourselves. Dear student
of misfortune, I submit: in an age when
everything is permissible, we were happier
when we were miserable.

It is the hour of the fridge-hum, the minute
of the weeping wallpaper, the second of
the second glass of wine—if I were drinking.
But let's indulge instead in pure invention.
As the world began, a singular light stuttered,
opened its spectral fan. Grey could have been
a glimmer in the peacock's plume, but

too heavy for the desert sky, too dour
for the rainbow, it fell into the corner of this room.
Now I feed it scraps of my Sunday afternoons
where tedium is borne on the backs of dust motes—
one by one, each to each, next to weightless.
Such is the fate of the despondent, to seek company,
wanted only by the unwanted.

I'm on a self-improvement kick: I've mastered charm
and now it's on to cunning and ruthlessness.
Here's my advice: once you've satisfied the urge
to travel farther than your own endurance,
go trade your existentialism for the blues.
This occurred to me in trickles, trembles, and one
vertiginous leap. I'm willing to show you,

though there is no pure evidence for anything,
only a miserly circle of light closing its mouth
around every sentient being. How shall I demonstrate?
In the evenings, a blizzard of starlings descends,
a debauched madness in the canopies of trees,
shrill notes come to insult the stillness: reminder
of your ten thousand wasted lives.

It is likely I am poisoning the houseplants
with cigarette smoke and sinister vibrations.
The sun comes out, then disappears, an eternal game
of peekaboo, whimsical winking of fortune
and misfortune, rumours of rain or voices
purling deep within cubist cathedrals
of Precambrian stone.

Stumble-footed, elevated, am I pilgrim here
or impostor? Regardless, each morning I eat
my synthetic breakfast, desiring the city's switch
and shift of contours, its multiple frames
of reference—thinking, brother, sister, I'd rather
have a loyal friend, or better yet, fall in love
with a stranger, with estrangement.

To move forward is to throw everything away.
I once barricaded myself indoors with revisions.
My Leninist cat would refute whole histories
just by winking her one cataract-eye.
This was when I was still on speaking terms
with my life, and believed in what it said. Then
the times changed. They multiplied, divided,

spiralled, and fractured, while the years spun off
like kaleidoscope pixels, pollinated the dust with shiny
new dust. Which is to say, rearrangement became
my doing and undoing. Old neuroses were healed
as new ones were named—as I strove in my thinking,
as I staged my campaigns. Believing whatever is meant
by *whatever means necessary.*

—⚇—

I can't tell you how it is I'm here—marooned!
Without compass, flag, or crew. Bad luck
stitched into the webbing of my sails. Sober
as a stump. Just as movement through this
mushroom-coloured funk suggests a certain
threshold I'm too familiar with—the line
beyond the shore, between bay and breakers.

The static craft only worsens over time:
the way things edited have no spleen to squeeze—
pallid replicas of a former voyage, seething in empty
flood plains of the signified. So be grateful
when you arrive, a tourist to sight the palisades.
Spying only seagulls on invisible strings.
The early morning moon in shipwreck.

I search the dictionary for hidden
meanings—how we can know whether we know
more than we think. But in the academies,
pathetic stains of language, odours of scholarship
kill the mood—with such indelible reasoning!
Only the authors, if they were here, might
speak of it, one of whom I watched

fall inside the light: a solid fact
whirled to myth, a skull assuming her place
in the implacable window glass, her name
a mnemonic latch. Now a breeze
crosses the hallway with pages in its teeth:
molecular event without consequence
until it is ascribed to a feeling.

The weather bleeds through, a dirty
rock-dove light, and I want the mist of breezes
salted by a coast where those who gather
polish their gaze like a bead of glass against the tide.
But I am either lost or hidden beneath the sky's
cast iron lid, a burble in the stew. Is there no place new
to go, no movement beyond a fixed perspective?

Here the ocean must be lamented in order
to exist—ocean words of these desert nights
crystallized on every page. While I become more
secretive, resentments written like rivers drying
from the corners of my eyes. Submerged
within this conformist climate which I accentuate,
in order to stay pure, with my disguises.

—〰—

Such new ways of thinking! But to pay the bills
my ignorance puts on its steel-toed boots.
Appeals to reason fall out of season, and still
I expect a miracle, or a warmongering hullabaloo
like some howling Saint Bernard—all slobber and mange
but affable when it finds a fresh bone to chew.
O, let's go where the music's loud and new,

surrender to the latest spiritual craze.
I'm not sensitive, just touchy, flitting between
art and politics, sex and death. And as we curl
the lines of logic, and the options of self-inflicted
violence are remorselessly pursued, so the ugly-seed
takes root. And as the Generals predicted,
we'll soon have all the money in the world.

I am channelling the monkey spirit
from the perfumed realm of the scimitar.
I am crashing my little cymbals, gyrating my hips,
and disobeying orders come from a place
that refuses to equate politics and
death. Here's to copulating and coping
with financial anguish. Here's to each

tiny stress-crack held together with
platitudinous cement (the History Channel's
retrospective cud, or my ignominious ancestry
muffled with blood?) Though I'd like to report
we go on, despite this atavistic drift, regardless
of laying down our pens. Enamoured instead
with the workings of the weapons.

Empire of the candle flame. Sworn enemy
of the peculiar dark. Tell me about these
charges on my cellphone bill, describe
the invisible transmission of waves, of space
billowing in between. You are like that certain
word, the one that goes missing at the very
moment it's most needed to explain.

It's fickle, it's fleeting, it's truly what I meant.
Now you look at me like someone else's bride.
You remove the needle's eye from the figurative
equation, entangle me in narrative threads.
Mother of all flickering, bewitcher of the mind,
I'm bankrupt in the least specific way.
Please tell me exactly what I've said.

Lady, pour me another bucket of eye candy.
I'd like to lick each speck of glitter off your perfect sex.
According to etiquette we should mug for each other
like monkeys before an attack, irradiate self-doubt
by supporting the troops. Tell me, what good are poets,
flicking their reproachful cigarettes? They are gloomy,
those who cannot afford to accessorize.

I walk to work, avoiding eyes. Grumbles of traffic
like sour words lodged at the back of the throat.
Such a terrible mind—even before looking back
I begin to enumerate and label my future
shortcomings. This is what is meant by *livelihood*.
Forget nightingales. Ode to a lucrative contract!
Metaphor as fetish. The lust of the market.

Bass in the breast bone, chimes in the cerebellum.
Music adheres to logic like a velvet skin.
This is an evening of capillaries spidering with gin.
This is stepping out from the cavern of the senses,
what hovers between first and second guess.
My thinking, embedded in the common distress, neither
personal nor sweeping, only insinuates

like grains in a photograph, dodged and burned.
Now I'd like to introduce a narrative thread.
Now, a node of consciousness enflamed by the sounds
and touches of raindrops, ciphers of early spring.
Yet there's a pacing that permeates deeper than any
shameless or beautiful content. There's a pattern
of dark impulse wed to discipline.

I'm in another time. And now
another still. What sequence of events ensues
depends on what befalls the night before the news
comes down. I'm drunk on chance, uncertain
points of reference, a reporter in a war without
a way to tell the story. Without a way,
it's you I'm with, nights dancing

with nothing in my arms—the poem,
a slip knot, a body going through the motions
whose only ending is to endlessly return.
And the dominion of the self subsumed
within the creation of the self anew.
And what stirs inside, a reason to endure
when reasoning runs dry.

The body's reach: this morning we
awake to someone dragging a mountain
towards the airport and a rattling chandelier
of birds. Overnight, leaves have articulated
the dreams of every branch and twig.
Palm fronds move as thinking hands
unfold a crumpled sheet.

Or a world inside the world, the touch
inside of touch we *are* but cannot feel.
Like the eccentric whose obsessions keep him
amongst his own small comforts and possessions.
How we pass at night beneath his lamp-lit window—
light spilling beyond its material frame
into other lives and ways of seeing.

Especially the Hand or Fingers
~ for Neela Rader

How touch travels
from person to person,
a series of gestures delicate yet
sure as a calligrapher's cursive script—
each ligature, an embrace.
     How a thumb brushes a knuckle
or strokes down a cheekbone—
esoteric sensation,
tacit instruction, flame
conveyed candle to candle,
a message learned by heart
and passed on,
mother to child,
     nurse to patient,
          lover to beloved—
its small succour proliferating
by means of an essential human need:
to feel our bodies shimmer, break
softly open, at once ourselves
and other.

Acknowledgements

Some poems in this collection originally appeared in the following journals: *CV2*, *The Fiddlehead*, *Interim*, *The New Quarterly*, and *PRISM international*.

Some poems originally appeared in the following online publications: *Coracle Press* (coraclepress.com), *Ditch Poetry* (ditchpoetry.com) and *nthposition Magazine (*nthposition.com).

"The Man Who Lives in the Gazebo" appeared in the anthology *A Verse Map of Vancouver* (Anvil Press), edited by George McWhirter.

Thanks also to the following people for their help with the poems in this book: Rodney DeCroo, Norman Dubie, Cynthia Hogue, Eve Joseph, Fiona Lam, Meghan Martin, Matt Rader, Jeannine Savard, and Russell Thornton.

Thanks especially to my editor Don McKay, and to my unofficial editor, Alison Pick.

Chris Hutchinson was born in Montreal and has lived in Victoria, Edmonton, Vancouver and, most recently, Phoenix, Arizona. His poems have been translated into Chinese and have appeared in numerous Canadian and U.S. publications. He is the author of the poetry collection *Unfamiliar Weather* (Muses' Company, 2005).